How Do I Stop Losing It with My Kids?

Getting to the Heart of Your Discipline Problems

William P. Smith

New Growth Press

www.newgrowthpress.com

New Growth Press, Greensboro, NC 27429
Copyright © 2008 by Christian Counseling & Educational Foundation. All rights reserved. Published 2008

Cover Design: The DesignWorks Group, Nate Salciccioli and Jeff Miller, www.thedesignworksgroup.com

Typesetting: Robin Black, www.blackbirdcreative.biz

ISBN-10: 1-934885-28-2
ISBN-13: 978-1-934885-28-4

Library of Congress Cataloging-in-Publication Data

Smith, William Paul.
  How do I stop losing it with my kids? / William P. Smith.
     p. cm.
  Includes bibliographical references and index.
  ISBN 978-1-934885-28-4
  1. Parenting—Religious aspects—Christianity. 2. Child rearing—Religious aspects—Christianity. I. Title.
  BV4529.S53 2008
  248.8′45—dc22

                          2008011209

Printed in the United States of America
18 17 16 15 14 13 12 11   6 7 8 9 10

Dinner is late again, and the living room looks like a failed disaster relief effort. You ask your son to put away his part of the mess, but he ignores you. You turn the TV off; he gives you a surly look. You say, "Don't ignore me, and get that look off your face!" He mimics you under his breath and doesn't move. Your face flushes, and you say, "I'm not going to stand for disrespect in my own home, and you'd better move fast if you want dinner."

He gets up slowly and mutters, "Whatever." Without thinking, you reach out and slap him. He stands speechless with surprise, anger, and embarrassment running across his face. Suddenly he's respectful *and* listening to you! You're surprised, but secretly delighted. It worked! Easy, quick, and effective! Who could ask for anything more?

Your conscience could, and it is. A small nagging voice in the back of your mind isn't letting you walk to the kitchen feeling guilt-free and good about yourself. Your slap seemed to "work," but you sense that it wasn't right. That's good.

Your unsettled feeling means your conscience is still alive.

Why We Lose Control

This story might not fit you exactly—maybe you never slapped your child—but haven't there been times when your child pushed all your buttons, and you said and did things that later bothered your conscience? Why is your conscience uneasy? Weren't you just correcting your child's bad behavior?

You are troubled because you lost control with your child. But *why* did you lose control? What was going on in your heart that made your child's actions so infuriating? The reason you lost control was that, whether you've thought about it consciously or not, your child was not fulfilling your desires. Let's take a moment to look more closely at what your desires were at the moment you lost control with your child. To help you, consider these questions:

- When you lose control because your child is disrespectful (or disobedient, or ungrateful, or anything else that annoys you), whose agenda for your child has become most important? Yours? Or God's?
- When you lose control, are you most concerned with your child obeying God's will, or your will?
- Whose desires (for peace and quiet, comfort, respect, obedience, etc.) are most important at the moment you are losing control?
- When your child disobeys you in front of others, are you most concerned for God's reputation or your own?

When *your* agenda, *your* will, *your* desires, and *your* reputation become more important than God's, that's a sign you are trying to be your child's god. That's right. Whether you thought about it or not, you want your child to treat you like God.

It's easy, as a parent, to confuse your agenda with God's agenda. God does think that respect, obedience, and gratitude are important. And God does call parents to hold their children accountable and to discipline them. But there is a bigger picture. Since God tells your child to respect you, isn't your child really disrespecting God (since he's ignoring God's commands) more than he is you? When you struck your son (or yelled at him, insulted him, pushed him, or knocked him down), were you thinking about your son's disrespect toward Jesus? If not, then the way you treated him was more about how he ignored your demands, than it was about his violation of God's commands.

Besides respect, there are plenty of other things we want from our children. Some of us want easy, comfortable lives; and our children take more effort, time, and attention than we want to give. Others of us want grateful children, who appreciate all we do for them. Maybe you want your children to excel and be the best they can be at everything they do. Or perhaps you only want your children to stay safe, and not do foolish things that will ruin their lives. You have your own list of things you want from your child. The list of things we want for and from our children is as individual as we are.

How a Desire for a Good Thing Can Be Bad

Some of the things we desire from our children are good things. But your desire for any of these good things—respect, comfort, gratitude, excellence, safety—can turn into an ungodly demand when you decide you must have it from your child or else!

To understand how your desire for a good thing can be bad, you have to understand the difference between *desiring* and *demanding.* You can picture this as the difference between open hands and closed hands. Open hands allow a gift to be placed into them; they're not greedy or grasping. You might be disappointed if you don't get a gift you really wanted, but it's not the end of the world.

7

The desire for your child to respect you is wonderful. It's the right way for children to live with their parents. You can pray that your child will respect you and let God know how much you would like to have it. But if you don't receive it, you'll still bless God and love your child.

Closed hands with fingers curled tightly around a thing announce to everyone, "I must have this or I die!" You believe you have the right to receive respect—especially from your children. "Look at everything I have done for you!" When you don't get respect you become angry—sometimes you lash out, sometimes you are filled with self-pity—but the bottom line is that you are angry.

Respect as a desire is a good thing. Respect as a demand is an evil thing. When you treat respect as something owed to you, then you expect it. When you expect it, you look to others to provide it. When they do, you like them. But when they don't, you punish them. You can tell when your desire for your child's good behavior has turned into an ungodly

8

demand by the way you react when she does something wrong. When our desires are controlling us and we don't get what we want, we often become angry and lose control.

Children's Hearts Are Not Won by Force

Parenting, as with every area of life, can tempt us to focus on obtaining some good part of creation instead of worshiping the Creator. The apostle Paul explains it this way: "They exchanged the truth of God for a lie, and worshiped and served created things rather than the Creator—who is forever praised" (Romans 1:25). When we set our hearts on loving what God has given us more than we love him, we are rejecting God and making ourselves into gods. When we make ourselves the center of the world and look for meaning, purpose, and direction in people instead of in him, we end up with ruined relationships (Romans 1:29–31).

How does this happen with our children? When you lose control with your children, you are communicating to them that their priority is to wrap themselves around you. They must give you what you want or pay the consequences. You are, in reality, demanding their worship. Instead of teaching them to live according to every word that proceeds out of the mouth of God, you are teaching them to live according to every word that proceeds out of your mouth (Matthew 4:4).

Such a warped world only works as long as your threat of anger and punishment is big enough to suppress your children's resistance. Sure, you can motivate with fear. People do listen and change their behavior when threatened, but only because they want to avoid the consequences, not because they desire to love and honor those in charge.

Consider what happens in a police state. Nearly everyone tows the line; only a few transgress the rules. But people are obedient because they don't want to be punished, not out of loyalty and love for their country. They are only biding their time until they can get rid of their oppressors.

Families work in similar ways. Children's hearts are not won by force. When your children are physically, emotionally, and socially mature, their true nature and attitude toward you will come out. You have taught them that their relationship with you is not built on Christ and his ways, but on you and your rules. When they reject your rules, it is likely they will also reject you, and you will be left without a relationship with your child.

Is there any hope? Yes, there is. Jesus came to free you from the demands that turn his good gifts into your selfish rights. He takes clenched fists and opens them. Jesus doesn't remove your good desires. Rather he reorders you on the inside so that your ungodly, twisted demands become godly, righteous desires. As this happens to you on the inside, the way you relate to your child will start to change also.

Practical Strategies for Change

Admit to God that your biggest problem is not your child's actions and attitude, but the desires that control you. Jesus says that we must start with our own hearts before we correct someone else. Here is how he explains this:

> Do not judge, or you too will be judged. For in the same way you judge others, you will be judged, and with the measure you use, it will be measured to you.
>
> Why do you look at the speck of sawdust in your brother's eye and pay no attention to the plank in your own eye? How can you say to your brother, "Let me take the speck out of your eye," when all the time there is a

plank in your own eye? You hypocrite, first take the plank out of your own eye, and then you will see clearly to remove the speck from your brother's eye. (Matthew 7:1–5)

Ask the Spirit of God (the one who convicts us of sin) to show you the "plank in your own eye." What is so important to you that you are willing to harm your child to get it? You can't discipline your child effectively unless you start by seeing your own sins. If you need help in this area ask godly friends, or even your children, to tell you where they see sin in your life.

Ask for forgiveness. Ask Jesus to forgive you for loving what he has created more than you love him. And—this may be hard—ask your child to forgive you. Jesus says that reconciliation is more important than worship (Matthew 5:23–24). Be specific with your child, so he knows exactly what you need to be forgiven for. You might not get a great response, but asking for forgiveness is extremely important. This will be the beginning of a new relationship with your child.

Open your life to God's people. The body of Christ helps all of us grow (Galatians 6:1–2; 1 Thessalonians 5:11). Tell your spouse and your close friends what you've done. Ask your pastor, elders, or deacons for their advice and help. Accountability to others safeguards your child, and helps you to stay in control with your child.

Make a plan for how you are going to relate to your child in the future. Here are some ideas for how you can respond to your child, without losing control:

- Refuse to let yourself spontaneously strike or yell at your child. You practice self-control with adults who sin against you; you can learn self-control with your child too.
- Take a mutual time-out. Say to her, "Sit there and think about what you did while I go and pray for wisdom. I will come back

and deal with this, but right now I need to ask Jesus to help me know what to do."

• Realize that you're not ready to speak or act until you understand how to direct your child to Jesus. You may need to call someone for advice before you deal with your child. That's okay. Give yourself time to think carefully before acting. Taking the time to consider how God wants you to handle disciplining your child will defuse your ungodly anger and make it possible for you to lead your child to Jesus.

Set positive goals. Don't just pay attention to your child when he is doing something wrong. Discuss what is going on in his heart when he is acting badly.

Your child's greatest danger when he sins is not from your anger. He's running from Christ and rebelling against him. Don't use God as a club to get your child to obey your demands; instead, help your child see the danger of disobeying a holy God.

You are on a rescue mission to bring sanity to someone in jeopardy. That mindset will allow you to combine concern for your child's safety with godly urgency. Look for Bible verses together that address heart issues, and memorize those verses. Role play with your child, so he knows what godly behavior looks and sounds like. Let him know in advance what the consequences will be if he misbehaves, and encourage him as you see him take fumbling, halting steps in the right direction.

Tell stories about your own struggles. This always gets the attention of children! Your stories will show them that you understand their struggles and will give them hope for change. Make sure you talk about your rebellion against God, the consequences you experienced, and how Jesus rescued you from danger. If your child can see how the gospel worked for you, they will have hope that Jesus will help them too.

Look for small ways that your child is changing. Since change doesn't happen overnight, work hard to notice when she is effortlessly respectful, and pay special attention when she is really working hard at it. Let her know you're paying attention, and you can see Jesus at work in her life.

Focus on one specific behavior over the next two weeks. Sit down with her and ask, "When I tell you to clean up, what's one respectful way you could respond? What one thing could you do or say that will let me know you care about my words?" Wait and let her think. Then encourage her to pray and ask Jesus for help. Thinking through her behavior on her own and asking Jesus for help will be more effective than any lecture you could deliver.

Depend on Jesus for daily help. Perhaps you are realizing that what you thought was godly discipline was really just you demanding your child's worship. Don't become hopeless about your parenting. Remember that, "if we confess our sins, he is faithful and just and will forgive us our sins and purify us from all unrighteousness" (1 John 1:9). We are forgiven and clean because of Jesus' death on the cross, and his resurrection is our guarantee that we can live a new life of worship. As you ask Jesus for help every day, he will make you into a parent who teaches your children to love and worship God.

If you were encouraged by reading this booklet, perhaps you or someone you know would also be blessed from these booklets:

Angry Children: Understanding and Helping Your Child Regain Control, by Michael R. Emlet, M.Div., M.D.

Breaking Pornography Addiction: Strategies for Lasting Change by David Powlison, M.Div., Ph.D.

Controlling Anger: Responding Constructively When Life Goes Wrong by David Powlison, M.Div., Ph.D.

Divorce Recovery: Growing and Healing God's Way by Winston T. Smith, M.Div.

Eating Disorders: The Quest for Thinness by Edward T. Welch, M.Div., Ph.D.

Facing Death with Hope: Living for What Lasts by David Powlison, M.Div., Ph.D.

Family Feuds: How to Respond by Timothy S. Lane, M.Div., D.Min.

Freedom from Addiction: Turning from Your Addictive Behavior by Edward T. Welch, M.Div., Ph.D.

Freedom from Guilt: Finding Release from Your Burdens by Timothy S. Lane, M.Div., D.Min.

Healing after Abortion: God's Mercy Is for You by David Powlison, M.Div., Ph.D.

Help for Stepfamilies: Avoiding the Pitfalls and Learning to Love by Winston T. Smith, M.Div.

Help for the Caregiver: Facing the Challenges with Understanding and Strength by Michael R. Emlet, M.Div., M.D.

Help! My Spouse Committed Adultery: First Steps for Dealing with Betrayal by Winston T. Smith, M.Div.

To learn more about CCEF visit our website at www.ccef.org.